JESUS

His 50 Most Powerful Teachings

Introduction

Dear reader,

In a constantly changing world, it is sometimes challenging to find stable anchors and sources of inspiration to guide our choices and actions.

It is when we are in this quest for wisdom and clarity that the words of Jesus Christ resonate with timeless strength.

In this book, I offer you a journey through fifty carefully selected quotes, each carrying a touch of wisdom that illuminates our modern lives.

But this book goes beyond merely presenting these sacred words.

The approach chosen here aims to make these teachings accessible to everyone, by breaking down each quote into four key elements: the quote itself, a simple explanation, a concrete illustration of its application in everyday life and a practical step to guide you in your transformation.

Understanding and Living the Words of Jesus: The 4 Keys

1. The Quote: each of Jesus' teachings is a pearl of wisdom. These words transcend centuries and guide us towards fundamental values such as love, compassion, forgiveness and hope.

2. A Simple Explanation: understanding the profound meaning of these teachings can sometimes feel complex, which is why we've taken the care to explain them in a simple and accessible manner. Each explanation will help you grasp the underlying message and put it into perspective in your own life.

3. A Concrete Example: theory truly comes to life when put into practice. Each quote is accompanied by a concrete example of its application in an everyday situation. These examples illustrate how Jesus' teachings can influence our actions, decisions and relationships.

4. The Application: a "Practical Application" section will guide you in integrating these teachings into your own reality.

This book is not just an exploration of spirituality, but also a practical guide to live with greater clarity, kindness and love.

It will serve as a compass for those seeking profound meaning in their existence and offer invaluable assistance to those facing challenges, opening a gateway to inspiration and transformation.

Even for those who are not currently facing obstacles, this compilation will be an extraordinary source of timeless teachings to continue evolving and discovering ways to enrich all aspects of life.

Whether you are already familiar with Jesus' teachings or encountering them for the first time, I hope this book will provide you with fresh and inspiring perspectives to navigate more confidently your own life.

Get ready to embark on a journey of enlightenment, personal exploration and transformation.

Jesus' words are like stars guiding us through darkness, illuminating our lives with their eternal wisdom.

Gratefully yours,

Martin

Jesus, The Story of an Influence

Jesus Christ, a central and profoundly influential figure in the history of humanity, is widely recognized for his inspiring teachings and his ability to touch the hearts of those who encountered him.

Born in the city of Bethlehem about 2,000 years ago, his humble origins did not predict the extent of his impact on the world.

From a young age, incredible anecdotes testify to his exceptional wisdom.

It is said that at the age of 12, he was already teaching and asking intriguing questions to rabbis in the temple of Jerusalem.

His deep understanding of scriptures and his ability to engage with scholars left an indelible mark.

Jesus' ministry was marked by acts of compassion and healing that defy comprehension. Stories tell of him turning water into wine at a wedding in Cana, illustrating his ability to evoke wonder even in the simplest moments of life.

His healing miracles, from restoring sight to curing lepers, showcased his boundless compassion for the suffering.

The parables he shared, like that of the Good Samaritan and the Prodigal Son, revealed his mastery of the art of storytelling to convey deep and eternal truths.

His teaching on unconditional love and forgiveness revolutionized humanity's understanding of spirituality and morality.

However, his journey was not without challenges and conflicts. His denunciation of religious formalism and criticism of the religious authorities of his time triggered controversies and tensions that ultimately led to his crucifixion.

His ultimate act of sacrifice on the cross, followed by his resurrection three days later, is the most extraordinary, symbolizing hope, redemption and victory over death.

Thus, Jesus Christ remains not only a historical figure but also one infused with mystery, compassion and love.

His actions and teachings continue to inspire millions of people throughout time, leaving a lasting mark on spirituality, culture and humanity as a whole.

The 50 Most Powerful Teachings of JESUS by Inspiring Divine Words

Copyright © 2024 – Martin

Cover Design by Martin Bouyssou

Contact: **les50enseignementsdejesus@gmail.com**

His 50 MOST POWERFUL TEACHINGS

"Love your enemies, do good to those who hate you." - Luke 6:27

Jesus teaches us here that we should love and treat well even those who do not love us or do treat us poorly.

Imagine you have a classmate or a coworker who treats you poorly and is unkind to you.

Instead of retaliating by being mean in return, you could choose to show them love by being kind to them.

Perhaps this could help them change their attitude and understand that kindness is better than cruelty.

By acting this way, you are following Jesus' teaching, showing love even to those who do not love you.

Strive to understand.

Take the time to consider the motivations and experiences of your enemies or those who have wronged you.

Trying to understand their perspectives can help soften your feelings and pave the way for empathy.

Practice compassion.

Even if you disagree with someone, look for ways to show compassion towards them.

Compassion helps you see the common humanity you share despite your differences.

Extend a helping hand.

If the opportunity arises, be willing to make a kind gesture towards your enemies.

This could be as simple as listening to their concerns or offering your support in a challenging situation.

2

"Blessed are the poor in spirit, for theirs is the kingdom of heaven." - Matthew 5:3

Jesus tells us here that those who recognize their spiritual need and dependence on God will be blessed.

Let's imagine you're facing a challenging situation where you're unsure how to proceed.

Instead of pretending to have all the answers, acknowledge your vulnerability and seek help from God, others, or spiritual resources.

This openness to learning and guidance will allow you to find solutions and sense the presence of something greater than yourself.

By practicing this teaching, you open yourself to spiritual growth, humility and gratitude.

Recognizing your dependence on the divine and being receptive to learning, you can experience a profound inner transformation and discover a deeper sense of purpose in your spiritual journey.

Practice humility.

Acknowledge that as a human being you don't have all the answers and that you have limitations.

Be open to learning and spiritual growth.

Evaluate your priorities.

Take time to reflect on what truly matters in your life.

Avoid being swept away by material desires or superficial ambitions and focus on aspects that nourish your soul.

Cultivate gratitude.

Appreciate the blessings you have in your life, whether they're big or small.

Gratitude helps you recognize that everything you have is a gift and fosters a sense of connection with the divine.

3

"Do not judge, or you too will be judged."
- Matthew 7:1

Jesus reminds us here not to judge others in a critical and harsh manner, as the same standard may be applied to us.

Imagine that you notice a coworker has been rather cold and distant in the past few days.

Instead of assuming they are arrogant or impolite, take a moment to consider other possible reasons.

Perhaps they are going through a tough time or have personal concerns.

Instead of judging, take the initiative to offer a warm smile and engage in a friendly conversation.

Your understanding approach can create a more positive atmosphere and pave the way for open communication.

By putting this teaching into practice, you cultivate an attitude of understanding and kindness towards others.

By avoiding hasty judgments, you contribute to creating more harmonious relationships and fostering an environment where everyone feels heard and respected.

Become aware of your thoughts and judgments.

Start by being mindful of your own thoughts when interacting with others.

If you find negative or critical judgments arising, take note of those moments.

Practice reflection before judging.

Before jumping to conclusions or passing judgment on someone, take a moment to consider the situation from different angles.

Try to understand the other person's perspective and the factors that might influence their behavior.

Replace judgment with compassion.

Instead of judging, try to cultivate a compassionate mindset towards others.

Consider what might be driving them to behave in a certain way.

Compassion opens the door to better understanding and more positive relationships.

4

"Ask and it will be given to you; seek and you will find; knock and the door will be opened to you." - Matthew 7:7

Jesus encourages us to persevere in our quest for answers, solutions, and guidance.

Imagine you are searching for a new job. Instead of just waiting for job offers to come to you, start actively seeking opportunities.

Update your resume, send out applications, research companies that align with your aspirations.

Throughout the process, keep persevering and seeking chances to move closer to your goal.

By putting this teaching into practice, you embrace a proactive and determined mindset.

You open yourself up to new perspectives and personal growth and achieve your goals.

Perseverance and action will bring you closer to what you are aiming to achieve.

Identify what you desire or what you need.

Take a moment to reflect on a situation or challenge in your life.

Clearly identify what you would like to accomplish, resolve or attain.

Take concrete steps.

After identifying your desires, don't remain passive.

Take actions to attain what you are seeking.

This might mean asking questions, seeking information or taking steps to move closer to your goal.

Persist with confidence.

Don't be discouraged if results aren't immediate.

Perseverance is crucial.

Keep searching, knocking on the doors of opportunities and seeking help if needed.

5

"Flesh gives birth to flesh, but the spirit gives birth to spirit." - John 3:6

Jesus emphasizes the distinction between material and spiritual dimensions of life.

Imagine that you are immersed in your work and daily tasks, neglecting moments of stillness and reflection.

Become aware of this dynamic and decide to dedicate even just a few minutes each day for meditation or contemplation.

By doing so, you are choosing to prioritize the spiritual dimension of your life, which can bring you a sense of inner peace and deep connection.

By practicing this teaching, you acknowledge the importance of nurturing both material and spiritual aspects of your life.

By nourishing your spirit, you find balance and live more fully.

Become aware of your priorities.

Take a moment to reflect on the material and
spiritual aspects of your life.

Identify what takes up most of your time, thoughts and energy.

Invest in your spiritual growth.

Dedicate time to practices that nourish your spirit, such as
meditation, prayer, reading of spiritual texts, or
inspiring discussions.

Make it a habit to connect with the spiritual dimension
of your being.

Strive for balance.

While material aspects of life are important, ensure that
material concerns do not completely distance you from your
spiritual well-being.

Find a balance between your material responsibilities and
your spiritual flourishing.

6

"I am the bread of life. Whoever comes to me will never go hungry, and whoever believes in me will never be thirsty." - John 6:35

Jesus presents here a symbolic metaphor of his spiritual connection with those who follow him.

Simple explanation

Imagine that you often feel an emotional emptiness despite your professional success.

Take the time to identify what you truly feel when you are emotionally "hungry."

Then, seek out activities that bring you joy, peace and contentment.
Perhaps meditation, spending time with loved ones or engaging in creative pursuits can help you feel a sense of fulfillment and fill this void.

Concrete example

By putting this teaching into practice, you choose to nourish your inner needs with sources that bring genuine fulfillment.

By connecting with activities and practices that elevate you spiritually, you can experience a lasting sense of satisfaction and fullness.

Identify your sources of inner "hunger" and "thirst."

Reflect on what leaves you unsatisfied in your life.

What experiences, emotions or needs always seem to leave an emptiness within you?

Explore ways to nourish these needs.

Become aware of what brings you true satisfaction and a sense of fullness.

This could be creative activities, moments of connection with loved ones or even spiritual practices.

Identify the sources of nourishment of your mind and soul.

Take a step towards spiritual connection.

As a metaphor of the "bread of life," Jesus invites us to find a source of spiritual nourishment that fulfills our inner needs.

Explore spiritual practices that help you experience a deep sense of connection and inner satisfaction.

7

"Let the little children come to me, and do not hinder them, for the kingdom of heaven belongs to such as these." - Matthew 19:14

Jesus encourages us to embrace an attitude of openness and simplicity, akin to that of children, in our spiritual journey.

Simple explanation

Imagine that you're attending a conference on a topic you are not very familiar with.

Instead of adopting a closed or critical attitude, try approaching the conference with the curiosity and receptiveness of a child.

Concrete example

Ask questions, be open to new information and pay attention to details that you might miss if you have a preconceived mindset.

By practicing this teaching, you're choosing to embrace an attitude of openness, humility and wonder in your spiritual journey and daily life.

By cultivating a childlike approach, you uncover new perspectives and experience a sense of freedom and lightness.

Adopt an attitude of curiosity and wonder.

Make it a habit to view the world with fresh eyes, just like a child would.

Be open to discovering and marveling at the small things in life.

Free yourself from biases and judgments.

Children often lack the biases and judgments that accumulate with age.

Try to shed your own judgments and consider others and the world without preconceptions.

Practice humility and receptivity.

Embrace a humble attitude that allows you to learn from others, consider new ideas and acknowledge that you do not have all the answers.

Be receptive to the lessons that life presents to you.

8

"A new commandment I give you: love one another. As I have loved you, so you must love one another." - John 13:34

Jesus encourages us to practice love toward others in a deep and selfless manner.

Imagine you have a colleague who is struggling to fit in the team.

Instead of distancing yourself or passing judgment, take the initiative to invite them to lunch or participate in social activities.

Show them acceptance and openness. Your act of love and kindness contribute to creating a more harmonious and inclusive environment.

By putting this quote into practice, you choose to embody selfless love and attentiveness toward others.

Through compassion, service and tolerance, you contribute to building deeper connections and creating a space where everyone feels loved and respected.

Practice empathy and kindness.

Make it a habit to consider the feelings and needs of others with compassion.

Try to put yourself in their shoes to better understand their emotions and perspectives.

Look for opportunities to help and serve.

Identify concrete ways to support others on their journey.

This could be a simple act of kindness, assistance or emotional support.

Show forgiveness and tolerance.

Love involves letting go of grudges and resentments.

Try to forgive others for past mistakes and maintain an attitude of tolerance and respect of differences.

9

"If you hold to my teaching, you are really my disciples. Then you will know the truth, and the truth will set you free." - John 8:31-32

Jesus teaches us that understanding his words and seeking inner truth can lead us to spiritual freedom.

Imagine facing a difficult decision and feeling uncertain.

Instead of getting overwhelmed by uncertainty, take a step back and contemplate the spiritual teachings that could guide your choice.

By choosing a path aligned with your values and the teachings you study, you experience greater clarity and a sense of inner freedom.

By practicing this teaching, you choose to cultivate a close relationship with the teachings that guide you toward truth.

By remaining within these teachings and applying them in your daily life, you can experience an inner transformation that frees you from the chains of ignorance and illusion.

Commit yourself to studying and thinking.

Take the time to study spiritual teachings that resonate with you.

Read sacred texts, inspirational books or teachings that guide you towards truth.

Practice meditation or contemplation.

Regularly set aside moments to meditate on spiritual concepts or teachings that resonate with you.

Meditation help you deepen your understanding and feel inner presence.

Apply the teachings in your daily life.

Identify areas of your life where spiritual teachings could apply.

Take concrete steps to live in accordance with these teachings, whether it is in your relationships, choices or actions.

10

"Blessed are the pure in heart, for they will see God." - Matthew 5:8

Jesus invites us to cultivate inner purity in order to experience a deeper connection with the divine.

Simple explanation

Imagine that you tend to criticize others in their absence, even if it does not align with your values.

Become aware of this habit and commit to purifying your heart by replacing criticism with positive thoughts and constructive words.

Concrete example

By practicing kindness and eliminating negativity, you cultivate a pure heart that reflects your connection with the divine.

By putting this teaching into practice, you choose to work on your inner purity by eliminating negative influences and cultivating positive intentions.

As you establish a deeper connection with your true essence, you can experience greater spiritual clarity and inner harmony.

Practice regular introspection.

Make it a habit to reflect on your thoughts, emotions
and motivations.

Identify aspects of your life that might be tainted with
negativity or ego and seek ways to purify them.

Cultivate kindness and compassion.

Take steps to fill your heart with love and compassion
towards others.

Practice acts of kindness and generosity without expecting
anything in return.

Avoid duplicity and hypocrisy.

Strive to align your words and actions with
your deepest values.

Avoid masking your intentions or pretending to be someone
you are not.

11

"Let any one of you who is without sin be the first to throw a stone at her." - John 8:7

Jesus reminds us not to judge or condemn others, as we ourselves are not perfect.

Imagine you are witnessing a situation where someone is being publicly criticized for a mistake he or she made.

Instead of joining in the criticism, take a moment to reflect on your own past mistakes and the understanding you would want to receive.

If appropriate, step in to defend the criticized person and promote constructive dialogue rather than condemnation.

By practicing this teaching, you choose to foster understanding, empathy and forgiveness in your interactions with others.

By avoiding harsh judgment, you contribute to creating an environment where mistakes can be opportunities for learning and growth.

Practice self-reflection.

Make it a habit to observe yourself and identify your own weaknesses and mistakes.

This will help you develop empathy towards others and avoid harsh judgment.

Promote dialogue and understanding.

Instead of criticizing or condemning others for their mistakes, seek to understand the reasons that may have led them to those actions.

Engage in open conversations that allow you to explore others' perspectives and experiences.

Practice forgiveness.

If someone has offended you or made a mistake towards you, choose to forgive instead of passing judgment.

Forgiveness releases both the responsible person and yourself from the grip of resentment.

12

"Blessed are the peacemakers,
for they will be called children of God."
- Matthew 5:9

Jesus reminds us of the importance of cultivating peace and harmony in our relationships and in the world.

Imagine you witness a disagreement between colleagues at work.

Instead of picking sides or taking a stance, commit to playing the role of a mediator.

Facilitate communication between the parties, encourage mutual listening and help find solutions that satisfy everyone.

Your role as a peacemaker can contribute to restoring harmony and promoting a positive work environment.

By putting this quote into practice, you choose to be a catalyst for peace and constructive conflict resolution.

By fostering open communication, empathy and the search for peaceful solutions, you contribute to creating a world where relationships are marked by harmony and mutual understanding.

Practice active listening.

When interacting with others, take the time to attentively listen
to their viewpoints and concerns.

This can help defuse conflicts and promote
mutual understanding.

Choose compassionate communication.

When disagreements arise, avoid impulsive reactions
and hurtful words.

Opt for calm, respectful and constructive communication that
fosters peaceful conflict resolution.

Seek win-win solutions.

When faced with differences of opinion, look for solutions that
meet the needs of all parties involved.

Finding common ground can help prevent tensions and create
an atmosphere of peace.

13

"For all those who exalt themselves will be humbled, and those who humble themselves will be exalted." - Luke 14:11

Jesus teaches us the importance of humility and modesty, emphasizing that pride can lead to a fall, while humility can lead to elevation.

Simple explanation

Concrete example

Imagine that you have received a promotion at work.

Instead of highlighting your accomplishments, choose to thank your colleagues for their support and remain humble in your interactions.

By doing so, you demonstrate that you value the importance of humility and recognizing others.

By putting this teaching into practice, you choose to adopt an attitude of humility that allows you to grow spiritually and personally.

By elevating yourself through humility and selfless service, you create a space for positive relationships and your own inner development.

Practice humility in your achievements.

When you reach a goal or receive recognition, avoid boasting or becoming prideful.

Remain grateful to others who have contributed to your success and stay open to continuous growth.

Cultivate an attitude of service.

Look for opportunities to serve others without expecting recognition or reward.

When you act for the well-being of others, you develop deep humility.

Learn from your mistakes.

When you make mistakes or experience failures, see them as opportunities to learn and grow.

Humility will enable you to accept your imperfections and work towards improvement.

14

"Therefore do not worry about tomorrow, for tomorrow will worry about itself. Each day has enough trouble of its own." - Matthew 6:34

Jesus encourages us to live in the present and not to be obsessed with worries and uncertainties of the future.

Simple explanation

Imagine you're worried about a presentation you have to make next week.

Instead of letting anxiety overwhelm you, take concrete steps to prepare for the presentation, like organizing your ideas and creating a plan.

Then, remind yourself to stay in the present moment and not let anticipated worries prevent you from enjoying the opportunities of the present.

Concrete example

By practicing this teaching , you choose to live with less anxiety and stress by focusing on the present moment.

By tackling challenges one day at a time and cultivating an attitude of gratitude, you can experience greater inner peace and serenity.

Practice mindfulness.

Make it a habit to anchor yourself in the present moment, focusing on what is happening here and now.

This helps you avoid getting lost in future worries.

Manage your concerns constructively.

When you worry about an upcoming situation, take a moment to assess whether your worry is based on concrete facts or imaginary scenarios.

Take concrete steps to address legitimate concerns.

Practice daily gratitude.

Each day, take time to acknowledge the positive aspects of your current life.

This can help you cultivate a positive mindset and reduce anxiety related to the future.

15

"I have not come to call the righteous, but sinners to repentance." - Luke 5:32

Jesus came to help people who have made mistakes and are imperfect, rather than those who consider themselves perfect. He encourages people to acknowledge their mistakes and change their behavior.

Let's say you had a disagreement with a close friend due to a misunderstanding.

Instead of holding onto your pride and refusing to acknowledge your own mistake, you choose to put into practice Jesus' teaching.

You humbly admit your share of responsibility in the conflict, offer sincere apologies, and seek to mend the relationship.

This honest and compassionate approach allows you to strengthen your friendship and apply Jesus' teaching that he came to help sinners change and improve.

Accept Your Imperfections.

Recognize that nobody is perfect, and everyone makes mistakes. Be honest with yourself about your own weaknesses.

Practice Compassion.

Show understanding toward others when you see they have made mistakes.

Instead of judging them, offer support and an opportunity for them to repent.

Seek Self-Improvement.

Identify areas in your life where you can improve and change for the better.

Engage in a process of reflection and personal growth.

16

"When you give a banquet, invite the poor, the crippled, the lame, the blind and you will be blessed. Although they cannot repay you, you will be repaid at the resurrection of the righteous." - Luke 14:13-14

Jesus encourages us to practice generosity towards those in need, without expecting immediate rewards.

Simple explanation

Imagine that you are preparing a special meal to celebrate an important occasion.

Purposefully invite people in need, like residents from a local shelter, to share this meal with you.

By doing this, you're showing that your generosity extends beyond your usual circle and that you recognize the value of each individual.

Concrete example

By putting this teaching into practice, you are choosing to practice generosity towards those in need, contributing to creating a more compassionate and united society.

Giving without expecting anything in return brings you a profound satisfaction, knowing you are making a positive difference in the lives of others.

Engage in charitable actions.

Look for opportunities to contribute to causes that support
people in need, such as the homeless, the sick
or the underprivileged.

Offering your time, resources or support has
a positive impact.

Expand your circle of friendship.

Instead of only associating with people similar to you, commit
to getting to know and helping individuals
from diverse backgrounds.

Building connections with people with different experiences
enrich your understanding of the world.

Give without expecting anything in return.

When you provide support to those in need, do it selflessly.

Avoid seeking immediate rewards, but know that your
generous action will be spiritually rewarding.

17

"Thus, by their fruits you will recognize them."
- Matthew 7:20

Jesus teaches that the actions and behaviors we exhibit in our lives are the criteria by which our true nature and intentions are discerned by others.

Imagine that you are participating in a team project at work.

Instead of seeking individual distinction, you actively collaborate with your colleagues, share your ideas, and encourage collective creativity.

By doing so, you demonstrate your commitment to achieving common goals and your desire to contribute to a positive work environment.

By putting this quote into practice, you choose to evaluate yourself through your actions and highlight behaviors that reflect your qualities and intentions.

By cultivating positive "fruits," you foster an authentic and positive perception of yourself in the lives of others.

Cultivate integrity.

Make sure your actions consistently reflect your values and beliefs.

Be mindful of your actions.

Take the time to reflect on how your behaviors impact your relationships and the image you project.

Show kindness and positivity.

Look for opportunities to positively contribute to others' lives, highlighting actions that reflect your benevolent intentions.

18

"Man shall not live on bread alone, but on every word that comes from the mouth of God." - Matthew 4:4

Jesus reminds us that our existence depends not only on our material needs but also on the spiritual nourishment that emanates from divine teachings.

Imagine you have a busy and stressful day ahead. Instead of solely focusing on the tasks at hand, take a few minutes to meditate on a spiritual teaching that inspires you.

This spiritual pause helps you approach the day with a calmer and centered mindset.

By putting this quote into practice, you choose to acknowledge the significance of spiritual nourishment for your overall well-being.

By integrating spiritual practices and teachings into your daily life, you can experience greater inner peace and a deeper connection with the divine.

Nourish your soul with spiritual teachings.

Take time each day to read sacred texts, inspiring books
or spiritual teachings.

This intellectual and emotional nourishment enriches
your inner life.

Integrate spiritual practices into your routine.

Engage in practices like meditation, prayer, reflection
or sacred singing.

These practices help you feel connected to a deeper
spiritual dimension.

Cultivate gratitude and awareness.

Acknowledge the many blessings in your life and feel
gratitude towards the divine source.

This will help you cultivate a positive mindset and experience
a deeper connection.

19

"Truly I tell you, whatever you did for one of the least of these brothers and sisters of mine, you did for me." - Matthew 25:40

Jesus teaches that every act of kindness towards others is also an act towards him.

Let's imagine you see someone on the street who is hungry. Instead of walking by, buy them a hot meal.

By doing this, you show your commitment to the teachings of Jesus taking care of one of his brothers.

Putting this teaching into practice means recognizing the worth of every human being and acting with compassion towards the most vulnerable.

By doing so, you embody the deep values of love and generosity promoted by Jesus.

Cultivate empathy.

Try to put yourself in the shoes of others, especially those in need, and imagine how you would like to be treated in their situation.

Practice kindness.

Actively seek opportunities to help others, whether through small actions or more significant gestures.

Show generosity.

Share what you have with those who have less, whether it's material resources, time or attention.

20

"So the last will be first, and the first will be last." - Matthew 20:16

Jesus emphasizes that the order of priorities in the divine kingdom is different from what we observe in the world.

Imagine you are working in a team and you notice a colleague facing difficulties. Instead of judging or ignoring them, offer your help and encouragement.

By doing so, you are putting into practice the teaching of Jesus, recognizing the intrinsic value of every individual.

In embracing this citation, you are choosing to challenge conventional hierarchies and promote an egalitarian approach in your interactions.

With humility and compassion for all, you are exemplifying the significance of acknowledging the inherent dignity of every human being.

Cultivate humility.

Question your own notions of success and merit.

Be open to the idea that a person's true value is not solely dependent on his or her social position or status.

Give importance to others.

Take the time to listen to and value the opinions and experiences of others, regardless of their status.

Treat each individual with respect and consideration.

Show compassion.

Be ready to help and support those who are considered less privileged.

Share your resources and skills to contribute to improving their situation.

21

"What is impossible with man is possible with God." - Luke 18:27

Jesus reminds us that human limitations do not apply to God and solutions that seem impossible for humans are achievable through divine power.

Simple explanation

Imagine you have a professional project that seems difficult to accomplish due to various constraints.

Instead of getting discouraged, persevere with the conviction that unexpected solutions might arise.

Concrete example

Seek innovative ways to overcome obstacles.

By putting this teaching into practice, you choose to open yourself to the possibility that seemingly insurmountable challenges can be overcome through means you might not have initially considered.

This reflects an attitude of faith and trust in the limitless possibilities of the universe.

Cultivate faith.

Learn to trust possibilities beyond your human abilities.

Cultivate an attitude of faith towards challenges you might consider insurmountable.

Persevere in the face of adversity.

Instead of giving up when facing seemingly insurmountable obstacles, view them as opportunities for growth and improvement.

Seek creative solutions.

When confronted with complex problems, consider alternatives and innovative solutions.

Open yourself to the idea that unexpected answers can emerge.

22

"I am the resurrection and the life. The one who believes in me will live, even though they die." - John 11:25

Jesus states that faith in him transcends physical death, offering believers an eternal spiritual life.

Imagine that you are going through a period of intense grief.

Instead of letting yourself be overwhelmed by sadness, take refuge in your faith in Jesus and the eternal life he promises.

Let this faith guide you towards healing and acceptance.

By putting this teaching into practice, you choose to anchor yourself in the belief of a life that transcends physical death.

This allows you to find deeper meaning in difficult moments and embrace a perspective that goes beyond earthly limitations.

Cultivate a deep faith.

Develop an intimate relationship with your spiritual beliefs.

Seek to understand what it means to believe in something that transcends earthly life.

Find peace in difficult moments.

When facing the loss of a loved one or moments of despair, lean on your faith to find peace and hope.

Nourish your spirituality.

Engage in practices that strengthen your spiritual connection, whether through prayer, meditation or thinking of the profound meaning of life.

23

" Peace I leave with you; my peace I give to you." - John 14:27

Jesus expresses his desire to offer inner peace to his disciples.

Imagine you are experiencing increasing tension at work.

Instead of letting yourself be overwhelmed by stress, take a break to breathe deeply and bring your mind back to a state of calmness.

By practicing this regularly, you create a space for inner peace.

By putting this teaching into practice, you choose to embrace the inner peace that Jesus offers you and cultivate it in your daily life.

By creating room for tranquility and sharing this soothing energy with others, you embody the profound values of peace and harmony.

Cultivate inner peace.

Take moments to connect with yourself, meditate and free yourself from stress and worries.

Practice kindness towards others.

Share acts of kindness and harmony with those around you, creating an environment of peace.

Let go of excessive control.

Recognize that some things are beyond your control and adopt an attitude of detachment that fosters inner tranquility.

24

"Let your light shine before others, that they may see your good deeds and glorify your father in heaven." - Matthew 5:16

Jesus encourages us to live in a way that inspires and reflects divine goodness.

Imagine you have an opportunity to help a neighbor who is struggling to move heavy objects.

Instead of simply passing by, sincerely offer your assistance.

By doing so, you reflect the light of goodness and altruism that Jesus encourages.

By practicing this teaching, you choose to radiate kindness and compassion in your everyday actions, thereby creating a positive impact on those around you.

By sharing your inner light, you contribute to making the world a better place.

Be a source of inspiration.

Look for ways to show kindness and compassion in your daily interactions, being a positive example for those around you.

Share your inner light.

Do not hold back on your kindness, generosity and positivity.

Share them with others to brighten their day.

Show dedication to others.

Seek opportunities to selflessly serve others, contributing to a better world.

The Sermon on the Mount where Jesus delivers the Beatitudes

« Blessed are the poor in spirit, for theirs is the kingdom of heaven.

Blessed are those who mourn, for they will be comforted.

Blessed are the meek, for they will inherit the earth.

Blessed are those who hunger and thirst for righteousness, for they will be satisfied.

Blessed are the merciful, for they shall be shown mercy.

Blessed are the pure in heart, for they will see God.

Blessed are the peacemakers, for they will be called the sons of God.

Blessed are those who are persecuted because of righteousness, for theirs is the kingdom of heaven.

Blessed are you when people insult you, persecute you and falsely say all kinds of evil against you because of me. »

Matthew 5:1-11

Be joyful and rejoice, for your reward will be great in heaven.

In this excerpt, Jesus paints a moving picture of the blessings and rewards that await those who turn to the path of love, compassion and justice.

Each of these words evokes a deep emotion and a promise of inner transformation, providing a glimpse into the divine love that guides his teachings.

25

"For whoever has will be given more, and they will have an abundance. Whoever does not have, even what they have will be taken from them." - Matthew 25:29

Jesus emphasizes the importance of the productive use of the gifts and talents that God has given us.

Imagine that you have a particular talent or unique skill, such as the ability to paint, write, sing, or even a gift for teaching or empathy.

Instead of keeping this talent to yourself out of fear of failure or lack of confidence, take time to reflect on how you can use it to enrich the lives of others and honor the gift that God has given you.

This action is not just a way to develop your own abilities but also a means to positively contribute to your community and give thanks for the gifts you have received.

By following this path, you acknowledge and value the gifts entrusted to you, paving the way for a more fulfilling life and a deeper connection with others and with God.

Develop and utilize your talents.

Identify your skills and gifts, and commit to developing and using them productively, not only for your own benefit but also to assist and enrich others in your community.

Share your resources.

Whether you have time, knowledge, or material resources, look for ways to share them with those who have less.

This can help create a more balanced society where abundance is more equitably distributed.

Avoid inaction.

Recognize that inaction can lead to atrophy and loss, even of what you already possess.

Take proactive steps to contribute, grow, and consistently improve both your own situation and that of others.

26

" I was a stranger and you invited me in."
- Matthew 25:35

Jesus emphasizes the importance of welcoming and helping strangers.

Imagine you meet new neighbors who have just moved into your neighborhood.

Instead of just greeting them, invite them to join neighborhood activities or offer your assistance to help them settle in.

By doing this, you embody the teaching of Jesus welcoming strangers in a proactive manner.

By practicing this teaching, you choose to see every stranger as an opportunity for learning and connection.

By opening your heart and arms to welcome others, you contribute to creating an atmosphere of inclusion and kindness.

Cultivate empathy towards others.

Imagine how it might be like to be in the shoes of a stranger in a new environment and treat them with the same kindness you would like to receive.

Be open to diversity.

Seek opportunities to meet people from different cultures and backgrounds and learn to appreciate their unique perspectives.

Offer your support.

If you encounter someone who is new to your community or in need of help, reach out to offer your assistance and warm welcome to them.

27

"Do not let your hearts be troubled. You believe in God; believe also in me." - John 14:1

Jesus invites us to place our trust in God as well as himself.

Imagine you have an ambitious and intimidating professional project.

Instead of doubting your abilities, believe in your ability to succeed with determination and confidence.

By doing so, you are applying the teaching of Jesus placing your trust in both God and yourself.

By putting this into practice, you are choosing to rely on faith in God and your own potential to overcome obstacles.

This combination of inner confidence and belief in something greater inspire you to persevere and achieve your goals.

Show faith.

Embrace an attitude of faith towards challenges and unknown situations, believing that solutions will present themselves in due time.

Cultivate self-confidence.

Recognizing your own skills and abilities is crucial for having confidence in what you can accomplish.

Practice patience.

When things do not unfold as planned, maintain a calm and patient trust in the process.

28

"And when you pray, do not keep on babbling like pagans, for they think they will be heard because of their many words." - Matthew 6:7

Jesus advises avoiding empty repetitions and lengthy speeches in prayer, favoring sincere communication with God.

Simple explanation

Imagine you feel the need to pray for inner peace or seek help in a difficult situation.

Instead of mechanically reciting long prayers or repetitive formulas without real meaning to you, take a moment to focus on what you truly feel.

Speak to God with simple and sincere words, directly expressing your thoughts and emotions.

You honor Jesus' teaching by establishing a heart-to-heart relationship with God, based on sincerity and authenticity.

Concrete example

Commit to sincere and personal prayer.

Take a moment each day to talk to God authentically, sharing your thoughts, fears, hopes, and gratitude.

Use your own words and express what's truly in your heart, rather than relying solely on ready-made or repetitive prayers.

Reflect on the quality of your communication with God.

Consider how you address Him. Is it a repetitive monologue or a sincere dialogue?

Be aware of the importance of being present in your prayer, establishing a true connection with the Divine.

Cultivate an intimate relationship with God.

The goal of your prayer should be to strengthen your personal bond with God.

Every sincere prayer is a step towards a deeper understanding of your faith and a more intimate relationship with the Creator.

Recognize that in the simplicity and sincerity of your words, you find a powerful way to spiritually connect.

29

"I am the light of the world. Whoever follows me will never walk in darkness, but will have the light of life." - John 8:12

Jesus describes himself as the source of spiritual light and offers the promise of a life guided by light and truth.

Imagine you are facing a situation where the truth is obscure or difficult to discern.

Instead of getting lost in confusion, take a moment to refocus and connect with your own inner light.

You could meditate or contemplate to clarify your thoughts and find an answer guided by the light.

By putting this teaching into practice, you choose to embrace the spiritual light that Jesus offers and apply it in your daily journey.

Following this path, you discover a source of clarity, guidance and truth that illuminates your life and your path.

Cultivate inner clarity.

Take the time to connect with your inner self, illuminating your thoughts and emotions through meditation and observation.

Choose the path of truth.

When faced with choices, consider what aligns with your values and the spiritual light that Jesus embodies.

Share the light with others.

Be a source of positivity, inspiration and truth for those around you.

30

" Whoever finds his or her life will lose it, and whoever loses his or her life for my sake will find it." - Matthew 10:39

Jesus teaches that sacrificing one's life for him and his teachings leads to a richer and more meaningful life.

Let's imagine you are faced with a tough decision regarding a career opportunity that would require sacrificing precious time with your family.

Instead of solely prioritizing professional success, take into consideration the value of spending time with your loved ones and creating meaningful memories.

By doing so, you are choosing to follow Jesus's teaching of sacrificing a portion of your life to gain a deeper and more significant quality of life.

By putting this teaching into practice, you are choosing to invest your energy and resources in aspects of life that bring true value and a deeper sense of purpose.

By aligning your choices with your core values, you are creating a more fulfilling and enriching life.

Prioritize what truly matters.

Rethink your priorities and focus on what brings genuine value
to your life and others.

Be ready to let go of the unnecessary.

Identify aspects of your life that steer you away from your
true purpose and be prepared to leave them behind.

Invest in meaningful relationships.

Allocate your time and energy to relationships that nourish
your soul and contribute to your personal growth.

31

"I am with you always, to the very end of the world." - Matthew 28:20

Jesus reassures his disciples by promising them his constant presence, even through trials and challenges.

Imagine you are going through a period of doubt or insecurity.

Instead of allowing yourself to be overwhelmed by these feelings, remember the promise of Jesus' presence.

Take a moment to meditate or pray with this inner assurance.

By putting this teaching into practice, you choose to live with the certainty that Jesus' presence accompanies you every day, regardless of the circumstances.

Recognizing his constant presence, you find the strength, peace and comfort needed to navigate through the challenges and joys of life.

Cultivate awareness of the divine.

Be attentive to spiritual presence and guidance in all aspects of your life.

Find peace in uncertainty.

When faced with moments of uncertainty and anxiety, remember that the spiritual presence of Jesus is by your side.

Share this promise with others.

Reassure and support others by sharing the assurance that the presence of Jesus is accessible to all.

32

"My grace is sufficient for you, for my power is made perfect in weakness."
- 2 Corinthians 12:9

Jesus reminds us that his grace is sufficient to support and strengthen us, even in moments of weakness.

Imagine you are faced with a complex professional project that seems to exceed your skills.

Instead of feeling discouraged, remember the promise of Jesus' sufficient grace.

By approaching the project with confidence and seeking divine guidance, you allow the power of God to be accomplished through your weakness.

By practicing this teaching, you choose to rely on Jesus' grace when you encounter moments of vulnerability and uncertainty.

Recognizing that his power shine through your weaknesses, you access an endless source of support and empowerment.

Practice humility.

Recognize your own limits and weaknesses, accepting that you do not have to do everything on your own.

Seek divine support.

When faced with challenges or difficulties, turn to spiritual grace to find the strength you need.

Cultivate trust.

Instead of being discouraged by your weaknesses, have confidence in the divine power that work through you.

33

"Whoever wants to be my disciple must deny themselves and take up their cross and follow me." - Matthew 16:24

Jesus calls for self-surrender and dedication following his teachings.

Imagine you face a situation where you have to choose between your own desires and the ethical values that Jesus taught us.

Instead of yielding to the temptation of selfish comfort, make a decision based on kindness and love for others.

In doing so, you choose to deny yourself and take up your own "cross," following Jesus' example.

By putting this into practice, you choose to set aside personal interests and embrace a path of dedication and responsibility.

By adopting this approach, you create a life aligned with spiritual values and the teachings of Jesus.

Adopt personal responsibility.

Take charge of your actions, decisions and behaviors, aligning them with the values and teachings of Jesus.

Let go of selfish desires.

Release desires and attachments that hinder your spiritual growth and connection with God.

Choose the path of dedication.

Commit to following Jesus' teachings with intention and perseverance, even when it requires sacrifices.

34

"Come to me, all you who are weary and burdened, and I will give you rest."
- Matthew 11:28

Jesus offers comfort and rest to those who are weary from the burdens of life.

Simple explanation

Let's imagine that you *are* going through a particularly stressful phase at work.

Instead of letting stress overwhelm you, take a moment to rest and rejuvenate. Meditate on Jesus' teaching and imagine yourself placing your burdens at his feet.

By doing this, you open the door to comfort and inner peace.

Concrete example

By practicing this teaching, you choose to embrace the offer of rest and comfort that Jesus provides.

By taking care of yourself and entrusting your burdens to a higher source, you discover a path to peace of mind and revitalization.

Practice self-care.

Take care of your emotional, mental, and physical well-being by seeking moments of rest and relaxation.

Entrust your burdens to God.

When you feel overwhelmed by stress, place your concerns and worries in the hands of God.

Offer support to others.

Be a source of comfort for those around you by listening to them and offering your assistance.

35

"Follow me, and let the dead bury their own dead." - Matthew 8:22

Jesus emphasizes the importance of following one's spiritual path rather than dwelling on things of the past.

Imagine that you have regrets about a decision you made a long time ago. Instead of continually tormenting yourself with the past, choose to focus on what you do today to grow and move forward.

By doing so, you put into practice the teaching of Jesus letting the "dead" of the past bury their own "dead."

By embracing this teaching, you choose to free yourself from the burden of the past and channel your energy into the present and future.

Following this path, you create space for growth, healing and the realization of your full potential.

Let go of the past.

Avoid clinging to past mistakes or situations that are no longer relevant to your growth.

Be in the moment.

Direct your focus to the present, making decisions based on what matters now rather than the past.

Continue your spiritual growth.

Commit to following the path of personal and spiritual growth, avoiding being hindered by the burdens of the past.

36

"Anyone who wants to be first must be the very last, and the servant of all." - Mark 9:35

Jesus teaches that true greatness lies in humble service to others rather than in the pursuit of status.

Imagine that you are working as part of a team on a project at work.

Instead of striving to be the leader putting forward your own ideas, take the time to listen to others and support their contributions.

By doing so, you embody the teaching of Jesus serving others and setting aside your desire to be first.

In practicing this teaching, you choose to prioritize service and humility over the constant seeking of recognition and position.

By serving others with an open heart, you contribute to creating a more united and compassionate community.

Adopt an attitude of service.

Look for opportunities to help others without expecting recognition or reward in return.

Cultivate empathy.

Try to understand the needs and challenges of others and be ready to offer your help and support.

Share your knowledge.

Share your skills and knowledge generously to help others grow and succeed.

37

"I am the way, the truth and the life."
- John 14:6

Jesus affirms that he is the way to truth and spiritual life.

Imagine that you face a challenging career decision.

Instead of making a choice solely based on material benefits, take a moment to reflect on Jesus' teaching.

Consider which choice aligns with your pursuit of truth and purpose in life.

By doing so, you are choosing to follow the path of truth and spiritual life that Jesus offers.

By putting this teaching into practice, you are choosing to seek spiritual truth and guidance from Jesus in your choices and actions.

Embracing this path, you discover a source of clarity, direction and meaning in your life journey.

Seek spiritual guidance.

Turn to Jesus and his wisdom to find answers to your questions
and direction in your life.

Cultivate a life based on truth.

Seek integrity in your actions and words, avoiding deceit
and trickery.

Be open to transformation.

Embrace an attitude of spiritual growth, embracing the path
of personal transformation.

38

"What goes into someone's mouth does not defile them, but what comes out of their mouth, that is what defiles them. " - Matthew 15:11

Jesus teaches that it is not what we consume materially that defines our purity, but our words and intentions.

Imagine you are attending a professional meeting where colleagues are negatively criticizing a project.

Instead of joining in the criticism, choose to contribute to the conversation by sharing constructive and positive ideas.

By doing so, you are putting into practice the teaching of Jesus, avoiding "defiling" the atmosphere with negative words.

By embodying this teaching, you choose to cultivate compassionate and authentic communication, refraining from letting words escape that could harm others or yourself.

By doing so, you contribute to creating a more positive and harmonious environment around you.

Filter your words.

Be mindful of what you say, avoiding hurtful words, lies and hasty judgments.

Cultivate integrity.

Seek alignment between your words and actions, avoiding hypocrisy.

Cultivate kindness.

Offer words of support, encouragement and love to others, thereby contributing to a positive atmosphere.

39

"Blessed are those who mourn, for they will be comforted." - Matthew 5:4

Jesus teaches that those who feel sadness will be comforted.

Imagine you have recently lost a loved one. Instead of suppressing your sadness, allow yourself to cry and feel your emotions.

If someone around you is also going through a tough time, take the time to listen to him or her and offer your support.

By doing so, you are putting into practice the teaching of Jesus that acknowledges that sadness can lead to comfort.

In practicing this teaching, you choose to embrace your emotions with compassion, including sadness.

By sharing your support with others, you create a space where emotions are honored and comfort flourish.

Express your emotions.

Allow yourself to feel and express your emotions without judgment, including sadness.

Seek support.

When you are going through tough times, do not hesitate to seek support from your loved ones, friends and colleagues.

Offer comfort.

Be a source of support for others by listening to their emotions and providing a space of comfort.

40

" It is easier for a camel to go through the eye of a needle than for someone who is rich to enter the kingdom of God." - Matthew 19:24

Jesus emphasizes the challenge for the wealthy to detach themselves from material possessions and enter the spiritual kingdom.

Imagine that you have recently acquired a new material possession, like a car or an expensive electronic device.

Before becoming excessively attached to this possession, take a moment to assess its relative importance in your life.

Consider how you could use your resources to support more significant causes or needs.

By doing so, you put Jesus's teaching into practice of avoiding material possessions hindering your spiritual journey.

Concrete example

In implementing this teaching, you choose to cultivate detachment from material goods and recognize that true wealth lies in spiritual values and positive actions toward others.

By balancing your priorities, you open the way to a deeper connection with the spiritual kingdom.

Practice detachment.

Evaluate your attachments to material possessions and strive to balance them with spiritual values.

Cultivate generosity.

Share your resources with others and support causes that have a positive impact.

Assess your priorities.

Reflect on what truly matters in your life and what contributes to your spiritual growth.

41

"Do to others whatever you would like them to do to you." - Matthew 7:12

Jesus encourages treating others with the same kindness and respect that you wish to receive.

Imagine that you need assistance with a project at work. Instead of waiting for someone to offer help, volunteer to assist others with their projects whenever possible.

By doing so, you are putting into practice the teaching of Jesus creating a positive and balanced exchange of support.

In practicing this advice, you choose to embody empathy and kindness in your interactions with others.

**By acting as you would like to be treated,
you contribute to creating a positive environment where everyone experience mutual consideration and respect.**

Practice empathy.

Put yourself in others' shoes and consider how your actions might affect them.

Cultivate kindness.

Treat others with respect, kindness and consideration, creating harmonious relationships.

Be the change you want to see.

Embrace a positive and compassionate behavior, acting in a way that inspires others to do the same.

42

"No one can serve two masters."
- Matthew 6:24

Jesus warns against dividing one's commitment and allegiance between two contradictory objectives.

Let's consider a scenario where you have to choose between dedicating more time to your family and responding to excessive work demands.

Instead of stretching yourself in all directions, choose to prioritize what is essential to you, remaining loyal to your family values.

By doing so, you put into practice the teaching of Jesus by avoiding serving two "masters" with conflicting interests.

By applying this, you opt to focus your energy on what aligns with your core values and main objectives.

By nurturing integrity and avoiding detrimental compromises, you forge a clearer path toward the realization of your authentic aspirations.

Focus your energy.

Identify your core values and top priorities and concentrate your efforts on what truly matters to you.

Avoid compromises that go against your values.

Make decisions aligned with your fundamental principles, avoiding compromises that lead you away from your path.

Cultivate integrity.

Strive to be consistent in your actions and words, avoiding internal conflicts.

43

"It is more blessed to give than to receive."
- Acts 20:35

Jesus teaches that giving to others brings more joy than receiving material things.

Imagine you see a colleague struggling to complete a task before the end of the day.

Instead of simply continuing with your own work, offer them your help to finish the task more quickly.

By doing so, you put into practice the teaching of Jesus experiencing the joy of giving and supporting others.

In implementing this teaching, you choose to embrace an attitude of generosity and contribute to the well-being of others.

In doing so, you discover the profound satisfaction that comes from making a positive difference in the lives of others.

Practice generosity.

Look for opportunities to give your time, skills and resources to others.

Cultivate empathy.

Put yourself in others' shoes to understand their needs and concerns.

Cultivate gratitude.

Appreciate the joy you feel in giving to others and positively contributing to their lives.

44

"It is not the healthy who need a doctor, but the sick." - Matthew 9:12

Jesus emphasizes that those in need or facing difficulties are the ones who need help and support the most.

Imagine you see a friend who appears to be going through an emotionally tough time.

Instead of just moving on, take a moment to ask him or her how he or she is feeling and offer him or her your emotional support.

In doing so, you are putting into practice the teaching of Jesus showing that you are there for those in need of comfort.

By embodying this teaching, you choose to be a source of support for those facing difficulties.

By offering your compassion and assistance to others, you help create a community of support and solidarity.

Be compassionate towards others.

Pay attention to the challenges and difficulties others are facing and offer your support.

Extend your help.

If you notice someone needs assistance, do not hesitate to offer your genuine help.

Listen and be present.

Lend an attentive ear to the concerns of others and provide them with your presence and empathy.

45

"Because you have so little faith. Truly I tell you, if you have faith as small as a mustard seed, you can say to this mountain, 'Move from here to there,' and it will move. Nothing will be impossible for you."
- Matthew 17:20

This teaching of Jesus highlights the power of even a small amount of faith to accomplish great things.

Imagine facing a significant challenge in your life, such as launching a new business, healing a difficult relationship, or overcoming a personal hurdle like the fear of public speaking.

Instead of being overwhelmed by doubt or uncertainty, take a moment to reflect on Jesus' teaching about faith. Even the tiniest faith, akin to a mustard seed, can have a monumental impact.

This might manifest in small steps, like meticulously preparing your business plan, initiating an honest conversation in a strained relationship, or enrolling in a public speaking course.

By putting this teaching into practice, you decide to strengthen your faith and integrate it into your daily actions and decisions.

Each small step becomes an act of faith, reinforcing your belief that even the most daunting challenges can be overcome.

Cultivate daily faith, even if small.

Start each day with a moment of reflection, where you nourish your faith, even if it seems as minimal as a mustard seed.

Recognize the small moments of faith in your daily life and give them importance.

Practice perseverance in the face of doubt.

When faced with challenges or situations that seem insurmountable, remember that even a small amount of faith can move mountains.

Use these moments to strengthen your faith, believing that you can overcome obstacles.

Use faith as a source of action.

Let your faith, no matter how small, guide your actions.

Whether in personal, professional decisions, or in your interactions with others, let your faith positively influence your choices and actions.

Faith leads to significant achievements.

By practicing this belief, you will discover that your faith, even if small, can lead to remarkable changes in your life and that of others.

In doing so, you experience the transformative power of true faith.

46

"Greater love has no one than this: to lay down one's life for one's friends." - John 15:13

Jesus teaches that the deepest love involves sacrificing for the well-being and happiness of friends.

Suppose one of your friends is facing financial difficulties and cannot afford an outing that means a lot to them.

If you give up that outing to help your friend solve his or her financial problems, you are putting into practice the teaching of Jesus showing genuine and selfless love.

By implementing this teaching, you choose to prioritize love for your friends, being willing to give your time, resources and energy for their well-being.

By expressing this love through concrete actions, you build deep and meaningful relationships.

Cultivate altruism.

Look for opportunities to support your friends and loved ones, even if it requires sacrifices from your part.

Express your affection.

Show your friends that you appreciate them and that you are there for them no matter the circumstances.

Offer your time and your listening ear.

Be available for your friends when they need to talk, share their joys and their sorrows.

47

"Do not worry about your life, what you will eat." - Luke 12:22

Jesus encourages not to be overwhelmed by worry about material needs, but to have faith that our needs will be provided for.

Imagine that you have financial concerns.

Instead of allowing yourself to be overwhelmed by worry, take the time to review your finances, establish a realistic budget and identify ways to improve your situation.

By doing so, you are putting into practice the teaching of Jesus taking action while maintaining a positive perspective.

By practicing this teaching, you choose to cultivate trust and gratitude in your life.

By adopting positive approaches to address challenges, you contribute to reducing stress and living more peacefully.

Cultivate trust.

Trust in your ability to find solutions to the challenges that arise.

Practice gratitude.

Appreciate what you already have instead of focusing on what you lack.

Make informed decisions.

Plan and take actions to address your needs while maintaining the confidence that you will find solutions.

48

"In this world you will have trouble. But take heart! I have overcome the world."
- John 16:33

Jesus acknowledges that life can be difficult and full of trials, but he encourages us to remain strong by remembering that he has overcome the challenges of the world.

Imagine that you are going through a period of stress at work, with tight deadlines and high expectations.

Instead of letting anxiety overwhelm you, remember that others have also successfully overcome similar situations.

By adopting a courageous and persevering attitude, you put into practice the teachings of Jesus facing adversities while maintaining faith in better days ahead.

By implementing this advice, you choose to draw inspiration from the perseverance of Jesus and his triumph over difficulties.

By approaching challenges with courage and seeking sources of support, you navigate confidently through life's adversities.

Be resilient.

Approach difficulties with an attitude of perseverance
and courage.

Find sources of comfort.

Draw closer to your beliefs, positive relationships and passions
to find support during challenging times.

Draw inspiration from the success of others.

Seek out inspiring role models who have overcome hardships
and achieved success despite challenges.

49

"For the son of man came to seek and to save the lost." - Luke 19:10

Here, Jesus reveals his mission of seeking and saving those who feel lost and disconnected from God. His unconditional love and compassion extend to those who need to be found and guided towards the light.

Imagine that you encounter someone who seems lost and discouraged.

Instead of passing by, take the time to talk to him or her and show that there is hope and support available.

Your compassionate attitude and willingness to listen could help this person feel understood and supported.

By incorporating this teaching of Jesus into your life, you adopt an attitude of attentiveness and compassion towards those who are seeking to be rescued from the feeling of being lost.

Through your actions, you spread love and healing, contributing to Jesus' mission of bringing light where it is needed.

Be attentive.

Take the time to listen and offer your support to those who feel emotionally, spiritually or socially lost.

Reach out.

Show care towards those who feel isolated by offering a listening ear, a shoulder to lean on or useful resources.

Share hope.

Spread encouraging words and positive actions to help others find meaning and direction in their lives.

50

"By this everyone will know that you are my disciples, if you love one another."
- John 13:35

Jesus said that mutual love among his disciples is the proof that they truly follow his teachings.

Imagine one of your friends is going through a tough emotional time.

Rather than minimizing their feelings, take the time to listen, encourage, and offer your support.

By doing this, you put Jesus' teaching into practice by showing your love and commitment to others.

By applying this teaching, you choose to place love and kindness at the heart of your actions and interactions.

By creating an environment of love and support, you help reflect Jesus' teachings in your daily life.

Putting into practice

Commit to actively loving.

Seek daily opportunities to show love and kindness to others,
whether through simple acts of service, words of
encouragement,
or by giving your time and attention.

Practice empathy and listening.

Listen carefully to those around you, trying to understand their
experiences and feelings.

This can strengthen bonds and help you love more
authentically,
as Jesus taught.

Cultivate relationships based on love.

Root your interactions in selfless love.

This can transform the dynamics of your personal relationships
and create a more loving and welcoming community,
true to Jesus' vision for his disciples.

At the Threshold of Eternity: The Farewells of Jesus

At the foot of the cross, amidst the darkness that enveloped Golgotha, a poignant scene was unfolding. Jesus, nailed and battered, lifted his eyes towards the sky. Around him, Roman guards and bystanders mocked and spewed their venom. But in the midst of this turmoil, a voice filled with agony arose:

**"My God, my God, why have you forsaken me?"
- Mark 15:34**

The shattered words seemed to cut through the air like an echo of suffering. It was the cry of both man and the son of God simultaneously, expressing the anguish of all humanity at that pivotal moment. Yet, even within this darkness, the light of love endured. In a whisper of weakness, Jesus addressed his father:

"Father, forgive them, for they do not know what they are doing." - Luke 23:34

An offering of grace and compassion in a place of hatred and violence. One of the criminals crucified beside him broke the silence:

**"Aren't you the Messiah? Save yourself and us!"
- Luke 23:39**

But the other criminal, caught by the aura of this man in agony, looked up at Jesus and said:

"Jesus, remember me when you come into your kingdom."
- Luke 23:42

Then, Jesus turned his head, his face marked by pain and answered him with a soothing voice:

"Truly I tell you, today you will be with me in paradise."
- Luke 23:43

A covenant sealed in the shadow of death, a promise of hope for genuine repentance. Amidst the cruelty of the crucifixion, a scene of boundless grace unfolded.

In His final moments, Jesus offered forgiveness, redemption and the promise of eternal life.

It was an exchange of words laden with profound significance, a revelation of love and mercy in the darkest of hours.

Acknowledgements

As I close the pages of "The 50 Most Powerful Teachings of Jesus," I wish to express my sincere gratitude for having walked alongside me on the path of spiritual discovery. This book represents not only my journey as an author but also our shared quest for a deeper understanding of the teachings of Jesus.

I sincerely hope that the teachings shared here have resonated with you, bringing comfort, guidance, and a spiritual renewal.

If you have found inspiration and wisdom within these pages, I would be extremely grateful if you could share your thoughts and impressions by leaving a review on Amazon. Your recommendations are a precious support, allowing others to benefit from the enlightenment that these teachings can offer.

I also encourage you to share this book with those who surround your life. The teachings of Jesus are a treasure to share, capable of illuminating the darkest paths.

With all my gratitude for your presence and support,

May God bless you,

Martin

From the same author

Available on Amazon.com